This is 30

Meghana Vodela

BookLeaf Publishing

Presentation by *BookLeaf Publishing*

Web: www.bookleafpub.com

E-mail: info@bookleafpub.com

ISBN: 9789357696470

First edition 2023

DEDICATION

To my Ammamma (grandma),

Even as an angel, you remind me how powerful my voice is. Living our wildest dreams is an honor I will never take for granted.

ACKNOWLEDGEMENT

Thank you to all of my loved ones who support my endeavors, no matter how crazy they seem. Thank you for always encouraging me to live my best life.

PREFACE

At 30, you would think I would have some answers. In reality, I have just grown to become comfortable knowing that will never be..
Welcome to a collection of "poetry" reflecting the world through my eyes and the many lessons I've learned..s. I hope you find something you need as you traverse through your own journey.

 All the love and light,

MSV

An Apology to 16-year-old Me

Dear Baby girl,
I am sorry
I am sorry I continued to seek the validation of
those who were never worth your time
I am sorry I allowed you to dim your light and
convinced you that was the only way to survive.
I am sorry I cared so much about what everyone
thought but you
You were never too loud
They did not want you to see the power in your
voice
You were never too selfish
Pouring into yourself would not benefit them.
You were never too promiscuous
Confidence would have made you too difficult
to manipulate
You were never too much
Your light was too intimidating for the weak

Dear Baby girl,
I'm so sorry you did not know it then but
you were so perfect
that others were afraid to let you see it

Enough

I feel stuck
I am never going to make it out
Am I always going to feeling way?
Like the pain will never fade?
Will I always feel worthless?
Am I just not good enough?
What does that even mean?
To be enough?
Who even decides what's enough?
Why do they dictate the perception of myself to
my core?
Whose voices of negativity have I adopted as
my own?
How dare I let those voices echo?
How dare I let those voices ever rattle my soul?

I characterize what's good enough when I decide
enough and I decide that good enough is exactly
what I am
Every ugly word comes from a voice that I
recognize not to be my own
No matter how much I repeat them
They do not belong to me
These words may reflect
The insecurities

The pain
The trauma
That others have projected onto me
But these are not my words
They do not originate from me
Because I decide what's good enough
And good enough
Is me.

Sapno Ki Rani

Raven black hair
Defined long nose
Brown skin reflecting the sun's admiration
Thick eyebrows and long lashes
Contouring those almond Earth brown eyes

You are beautiful
Don't ever let them tell you otherwise

Appropriation

How dare you tell me to go back to my country
While you sip on your turmeric "chai tea"
So ignorant can't recognize the redundancy
How dare you tell me to go back to my country
When you just sweated off your overdrawn
eyebrows
at Bikram Yoga
Rushing home
so you can watch Bollywood movies and eat
butter chicken
with "naan bread"
So ignorant you cannot even recognize the
redundancy
How dare you?

1965

Model minority
What does it even mean?
They applauded
Tricked, and deceived us
While we conformed
Appeased,
Begged,
Uplifted,
Engaged,
Admired,
Coveted,
One way of life
One color to be exact
Even at the cost of betraying what was ours
And even worse, our brothers and sisters
They reached their hands out to us
While we stomped across their backs
They invited us to their table
While we took stole their chairs
And shut the door behind us
"Model minority"
Nothing but a myth
that models a scapegoat strategy
to justify turning backs on

our brothers and sisters
we are nothing but pawns used
to disenfranchise our minority

Neuro-"spicy"

My thoughts continuously unravel
The voice in my head never stops
but it also often fails to remind me of the
important stuff
My thoughts travel so fast that I forget most
things I've written down
"You're so organized", I'm told
I reluctantly respond thank you
Knowing that I'm seconds away from crumbling
That if I don't prepare 10x more
Have all my systems in check
Journals, calendars, alarms, reminders on my
phone, vitamins
I would completely fall apart
It always feels like I have to give 100%
Or I will have nothing to give at all
The burnout is so real
How does anyone give 100% all the time?
Falling apart is no option either
The anxiety hopefully leads to productivity
but can also lead to procrastination
because I want to be perfect
but I also need to get things done
but if I get nothing done
then nothing is perfect

which leads to sadness and anger
but even if I get things done
giving 100% with no break leads to burnout
So to you, I may just be sitting on my phone
but in reality, I've planned my entire day and
already forgot the first task,
have exhausted my entire brain, and I can only
scrape together the energy to
dissociate
Hopefully the thoughts stop unraveling
Hopefully they stop going so fast
But not too slow either
And they better not stop either
That makes sense…
Right?

WCW

WCW
I don't want to be appeased
I want to be valued
I don't want to be liked
I want to be valued
I do not want to be lusted after
I want to be loved

I don't want to be coveted
I want to be cherished
The heteronormative disconnect that plagues us
all
As women, we are required to take everything
"compliment"
while exuding our brightest smile and gratitude
While ALSO simultaneously expecting a sexual
proposition
as a follow up without taking offense
or responding with rejection
but also knowing we become whores upon
acceptance
Unsure of the incentive of welcoming a
proposition that is followed by
Disrespect

But also fearful of the life-threatening
consequences that come with rejection
Harassment, Abuse, Rape, Disfigurement,
Rape… just to name a few
So thank you for your interest
I guess I will have to accept
Even if I don't want to
Because I'd rather be disrespected and called a
whore than
Face the consequences unknown
I don't know if my rejection will lead to a
"You're ugly anyways"
Or the end of my life perhaps
Women Can't Win, can they?

A Bad Day

A bad day isn't a bad life
Nothing goes right.
Nothing goes as planned.
You try your hardest
For what feels like nothing
Chest and shoulders tight
Every breath feels like a gasp
It is a bad day
Do not deny that
But just remember
A bad day helps us truly distinguish
What is a good day
A bad day stands out because
It's not a normal day
But most of all
A bad day isn't
A bad life

Integrity

Karma is a lie to trick people into doing good
Good things happen to bad people
Bad things happen to good people
Not everything can be explained
Don't do good to receive good
Just do good

The Law of Detachment

Achievement cannot be a condition precedent to
happiness
If our happiness is contingent upon the
attainment of a goal
Then that happiness cannot be unlocked till the
goal is achieved
And even worse
That happiness is fleeting
Only lasting till the next ambition surfaces
A life where happiness is not contingent on a
condition
That is the happiest kind of life

The Myth of Perfect Timing

We waste our lives
waiting

waiting to finish school
waiting to get our dream job
waiting to find the "one"
waiting to get married
waiting to have children
rinse and repeat
taught that we aren't allowed
to be happy
till we checked off every item
on the life milestone grocery list

I refuse to wait till I am
on my deathbed
only then to think of all
the moments
I now realize are happy moments
but back then
were moments of waiting for
the perfect time

I refuse to wait till it's too late
to recognize that I am living
the exact moment I was waiting for

Lessons from my quarter-life crisis

One thing the universe
is going to do
is keep kicking your ass
Teach you
the same lesson
over and over
the consequences
more intense
each time
until you learn
the same demons
with different faces
the universe is going to keep kicking your ass
until you choose differently

The Beauty of Hitting Rock Bottom

The Beauty of Hitting Rock Bottom
Hitting rock bottom is terrifying
Because it's rock bottom
It's the worst of the worst
It can't get any worse
But that's what also makes it beautiful
There is only one way to go from here
What most don't realize about rock bottoms is
You choose where it is
You choose what rock bottom is
You decide what's the worst you'll take
You decide when things need to change
The moment where you decide where rock
bottom is
It can't get any worse
This is the worst it will ever be
That's the beauty of rock bottom

Resilience

A quality universally admired
We love a self-made (wo)man
We love a good underdog story
The paradox of resilience is
that adversity is necessary

Per Se

If nothing else,
I hope to live a life so abundant
I never have the urge
to even speak of it

Hustle

Contrary to what they tell you
Perfection is never the aim
Persistence is the real key
Because 10 bad steps get you closer
than waiting for perfection ever will

Prayer

Stop pleading
Stop begging
Stop asking
Stop requesting
Stop bargaining
Stop negotiating
Prayer was never intended
To be a petition
Rather it is a collaboration
A discussion
An understanding of a plan
A release from expectation
A proclamation of trust and faith
Prayer is what elicits the plan of the Highest
power to unfold
Prayer is not about asking the universe for what
you want
but telling the universe you're ready to receive
what is waiting for you

Home

I spent most of my life searching for "home"
The place I could feel safe
The place where I would feel love unconditionally
The place where perfection wasn't an expectation
The place where my authenticity would be accepted
My searches often felt like failures
Thought it was impossible for someone like me
The reality was that I was searching for these things
in a place
I was searching for a roof, door, and walls

But when I truly look back on this life, even with so
much left to live
I have found home many times
I've found home in the embrace of a loved one I have
not seen in a while
I've found home when my dog lays their head on my
lap after a long day
In the aroma of my parents' cooking
In the laughter and banter of a best friend
In a forehead kiss
In my own confidence
In the gratitude of a client's voice after a trial
It may not have always be four walls, a roof, and a
door
But I've found home abundantly